Table of Contents

How to use this book:

It is recommended that the first six sections of this book be completed in order, as they are designed to gradually build on important early learning skills. To reference specific areas of learning, use the Index at the back of this book.

Writing is part of preparing your child for school, which involves helping him or her to develop fine motor skills used in tracing and writing. The first section of this book offers pre-writing activities to strengthen these skills. Before your child is ready to write letters and numbers, he or she needs to practice controlling a writing utensil. You may wish to start your child with an oversized crayon, marker or pencil to increase hand control.

Letters teaches your child how to form letters correctly, building upon the skills practiced in the first section.

Numbers teaches your child how to form the numbers 1-20, and offers practice in addition and subtraction. The activities are designed to help your child grasp the meaning and method of these basic math functions and to sharpen problem solving skills.

Opposites offers your child practice in understanding the concepts and the language of location and direction. These activities help in developing spatial skills.

This book also includes interactive learning tools. The decoder is used on pages 83-160. Your child can use it to check answers once he/she has completed an activity. Cut-out flash cards are provided for numbers 1-20 on pages 107-110.

WRITING

Help your child:

- control a writing utensil
- practice fine motor skills
- practice pre-writing skills
- write different line styles

Make a scribble.

Make some zig zags. /\/\/\/

Make some curly lines. ᴓᴓᴓᴓᴓ

Make some straight lines.

4

Hi, I'm Dora. We're playing Follow the Leader—and I'm the leader! Will you help my friends do exactly what I do? Great, let's play!

I just walked across this log.

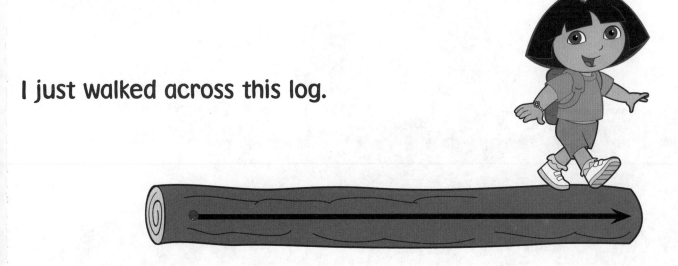

Help Boots and Isa cross the log, too. Trace the dashed lines.

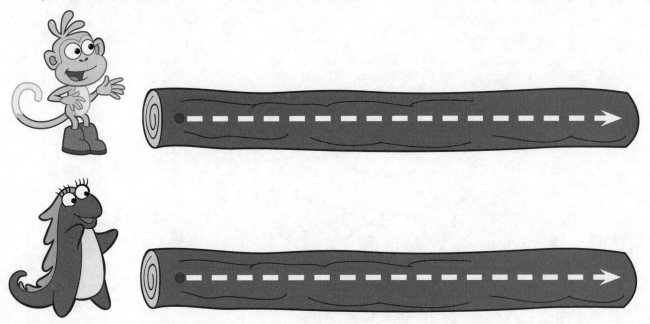

Draw a line from **A** to **B** to help Tico across. Great!

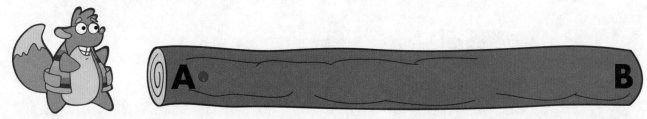

Everybody follow me! Trace the lines, and connect the dots from 1 to 5.

Connect the dots from **1** to **10** to finish the picture.
Color the picture.

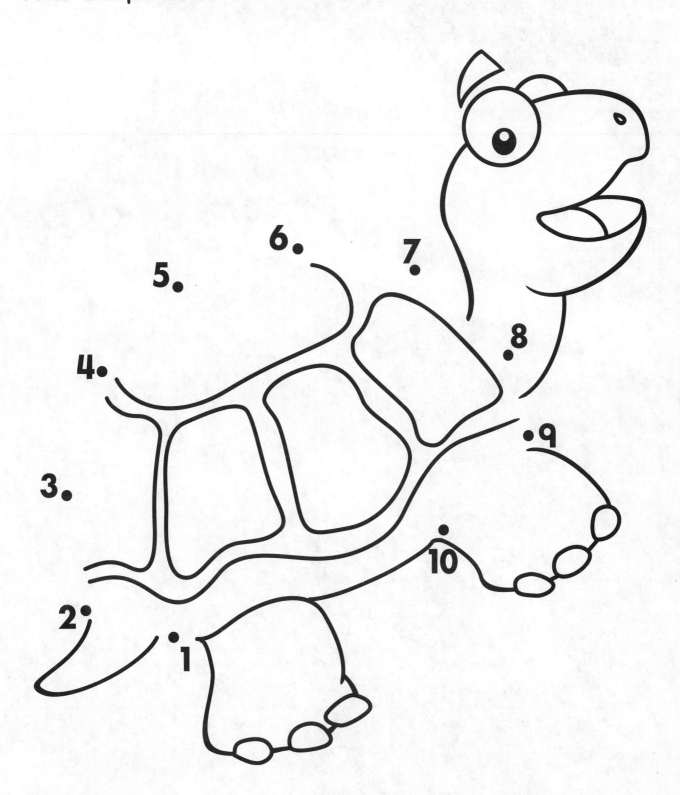

Trace the lines to help us crawl under this branch.

Trace the tree's roots and draw some more leaves.
Then color the picture.

Now Boots is the leader. Trace the lines to help us jump over the puddles like Boots. Then color the puddles.

Circle the sunny day things.
Mark an X on the rainy day things.

How can we get over these prickly branches? We can all swing on the vines!

Connect the dots from **1** to **10** to help me swing over the prickly branches.

Find the little plant that is exactly the same as the big plant in each row. Color them to match.

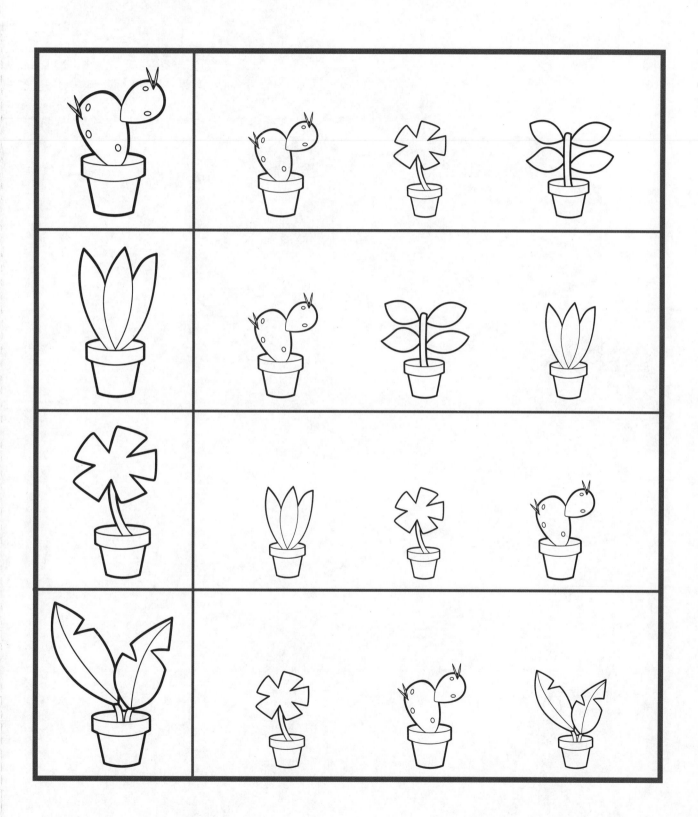

Now Tico is leading us over the rocks. Trace the lines so we know where to climb!

Count the rocks in each pile and write the number.
Match the piles with the same number of rocks.

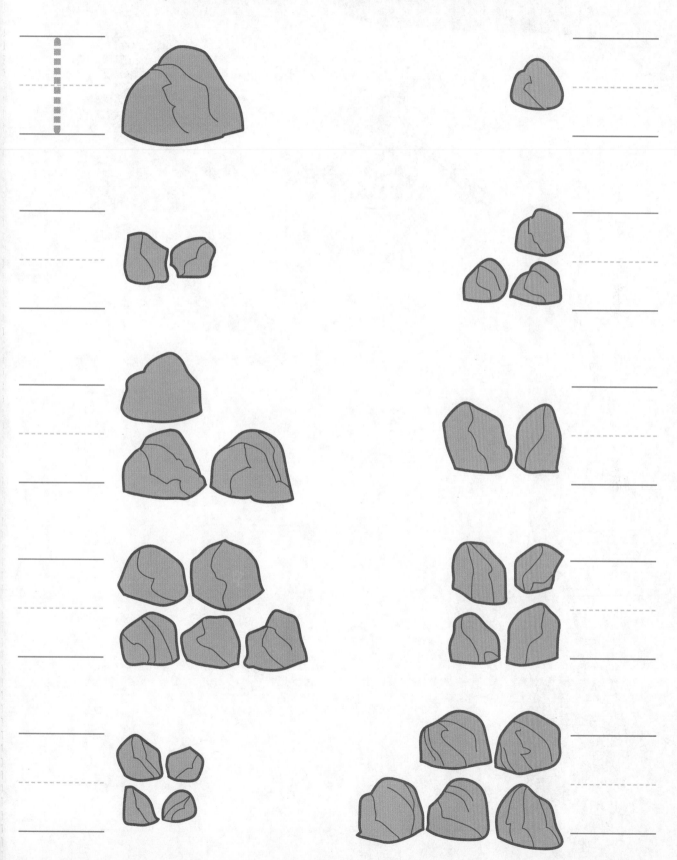

Let's follow Tico across the lake.
Trace the lines to help us row!

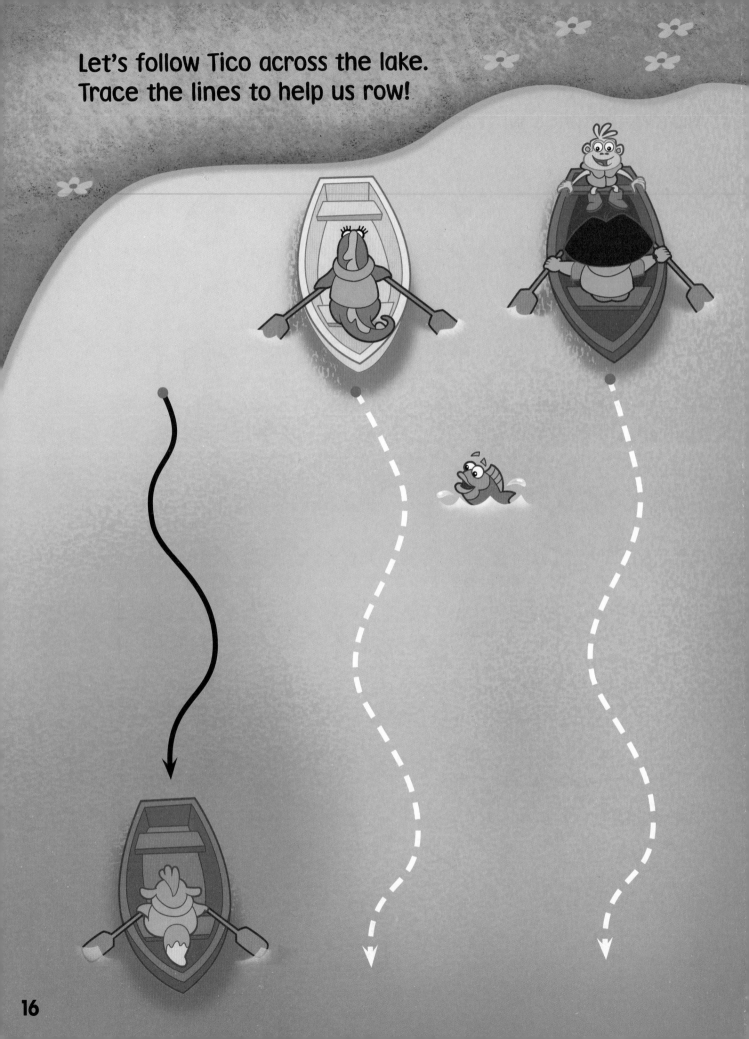

Help this fish find his friends.

Isa is leading us through a meadow. Look! She's dancing around the flowers! Let's follow her.

Help the bee find the flowers.

Quick! The leader is riding her scooter.
Trace the lines to follow her.

20

Draw a line between the toys that are the same.

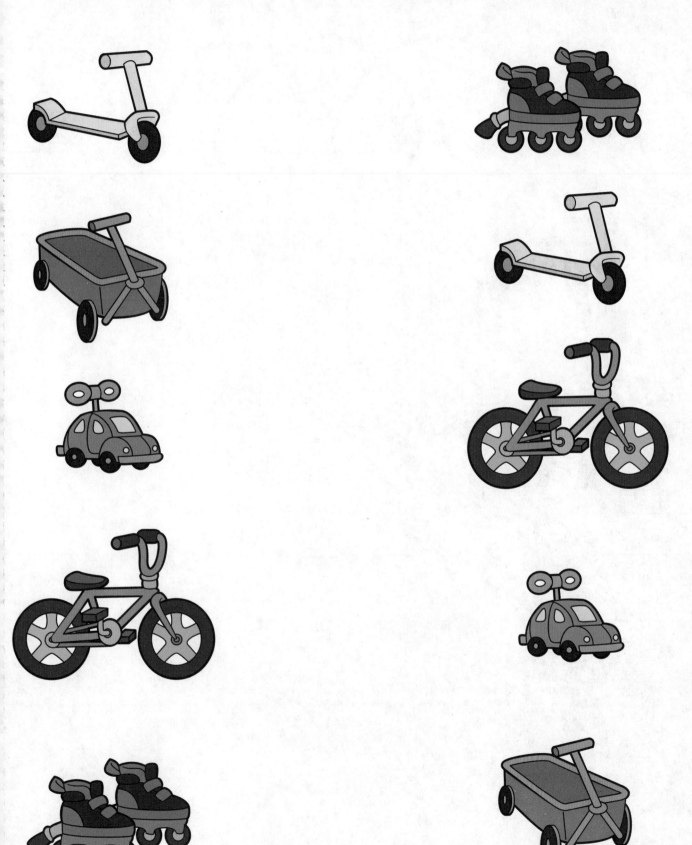

Boots loves to do cartwheels. Do you know how to do a cartwheel? Trace the lines to show us how.

Circle the butterfly that is different in each row. Then color the two matching butterflies in each row.

Now we're skipping across Bubble Bridge. Step-hop! Step-hop! Trace the lines, and connect the dots from **1** to **20**.

4   5   10   11   16   17
3   6   9   12   15   18
1   2   7   8   13   14   19   20

Trace and count the yellow bubbles. Then draw a path from the bubble wand to the jar.

Thanks for playing Follow the Leader with us! Let's play one more game! Will you help each of us get home?

Practice making some different kinds of lines on your own!

LETTERS
Teach your child to:
- identify upper and lowercase letters
- recite the letters of the alphabet
- understand that letters are made up of lines and shapes
- trace each letter of the alphabet

Write your name on the line.

Now write some of the other letters you know.

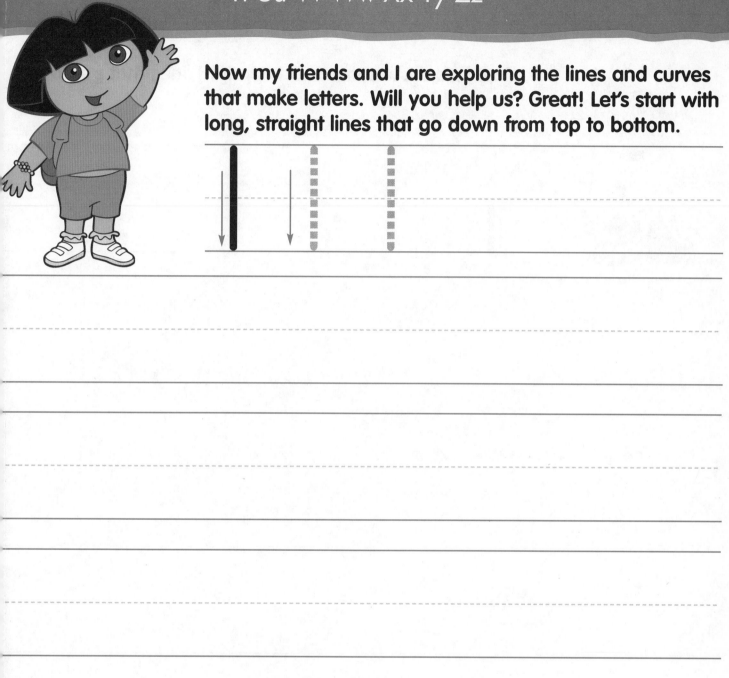

Now my friends and I are exploring the lines and curves that make letters. Will you help us? Great! Let's start with long, straight lines that go down from top to bottom.

Here are some letters that we can write with a long straight line.

Now let's draw some short, straight lines that go down!

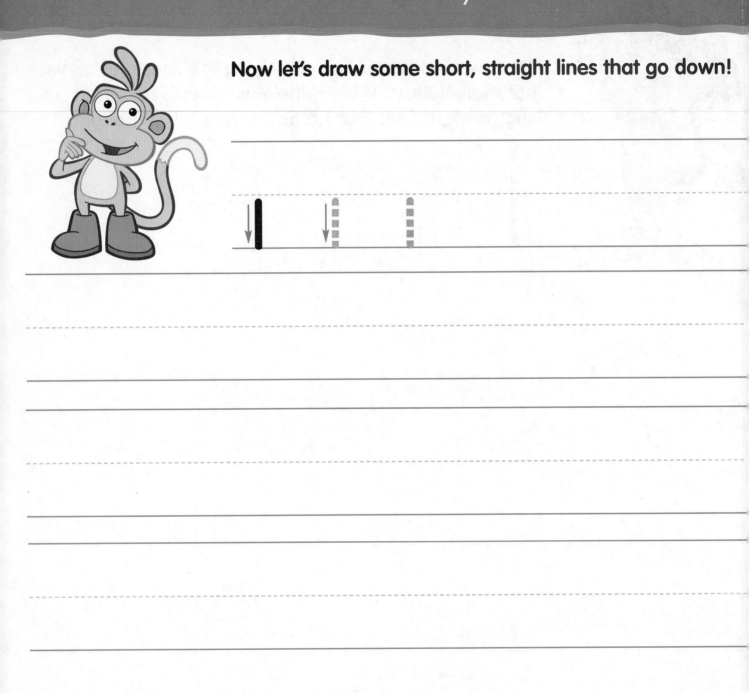

Draw the short, straight lines in these letters.

Let's try some lines that go across!
First, we'll do some long lines that go across.

Draw the long lines that go across in these letters.

Now draw short lines that go across with Tico!

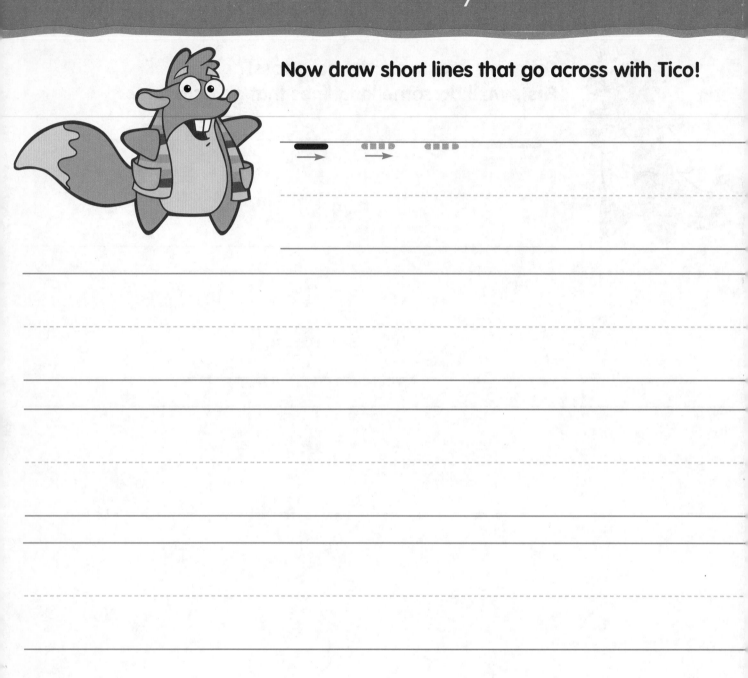

Here are some letters with short lines that go across.

Let's put it together! Write these letters, then finish writing the names of our friends.

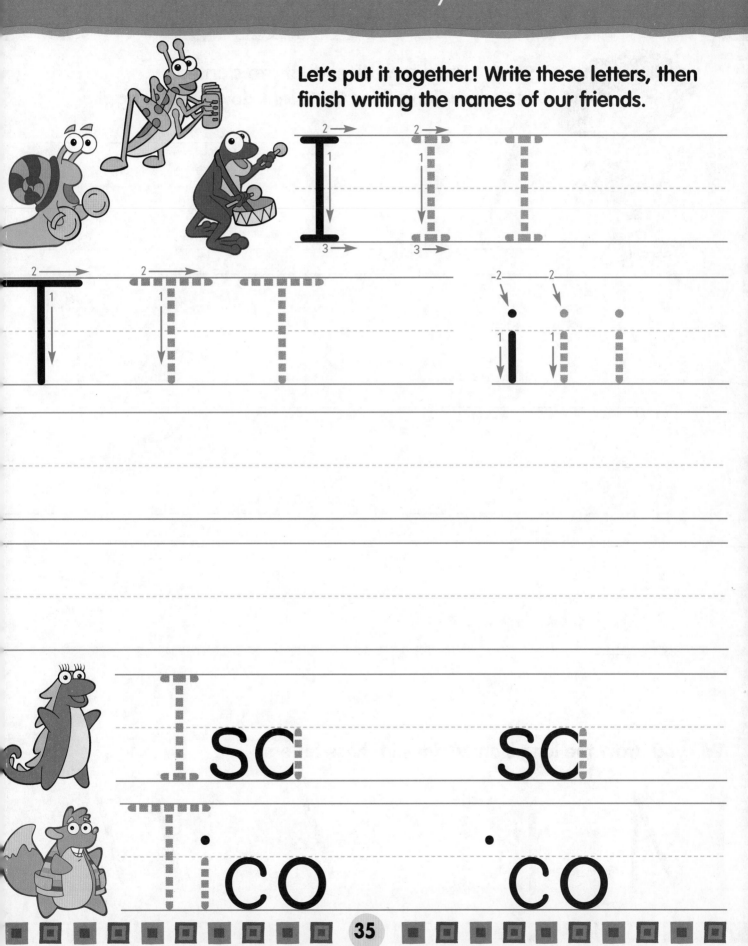

Some letters have lines that are slanted.
Let's draw long lines that slant down to the right.

Will you draw the long slanted lines in these letters?

Help Benny draw short lines that slant down to the right!

Here are some letters with short lines that slant down to the right.

Will you help us draw lines that slant down to the left? Great! Draw these long slanted lines.

Now draw the lines that slant down to the left in these letters.

Let's draw short lines that slant down to the left.

Here are some letters with lines that slant down to the left.

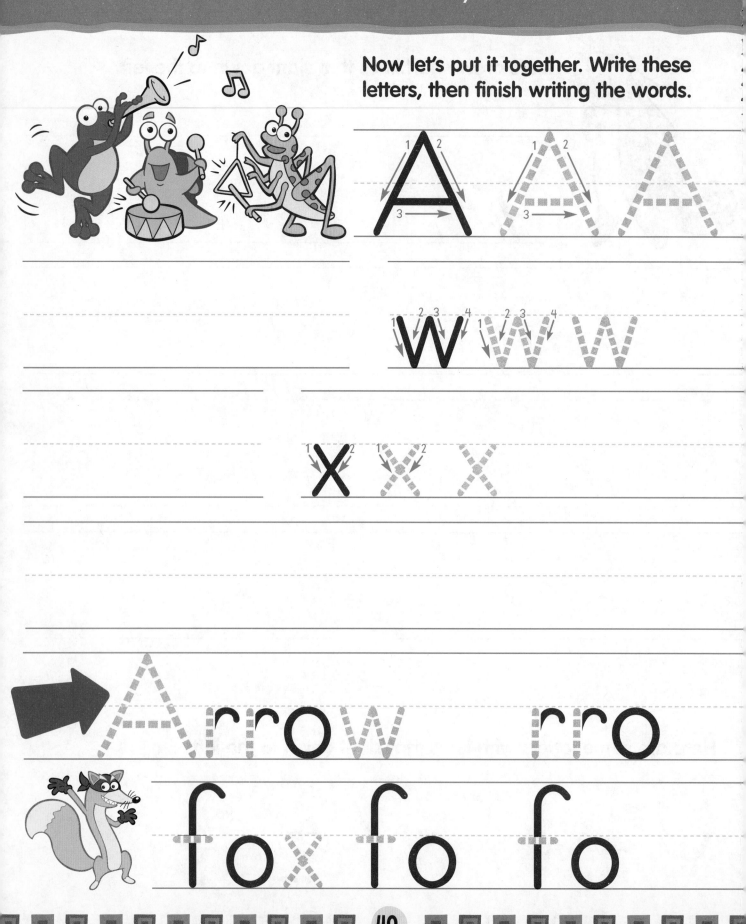

Now let's put it together. Write these letters, then finish writing the words.

A A A

W W W

X X X

Arrow   rro

fox   fo   fo

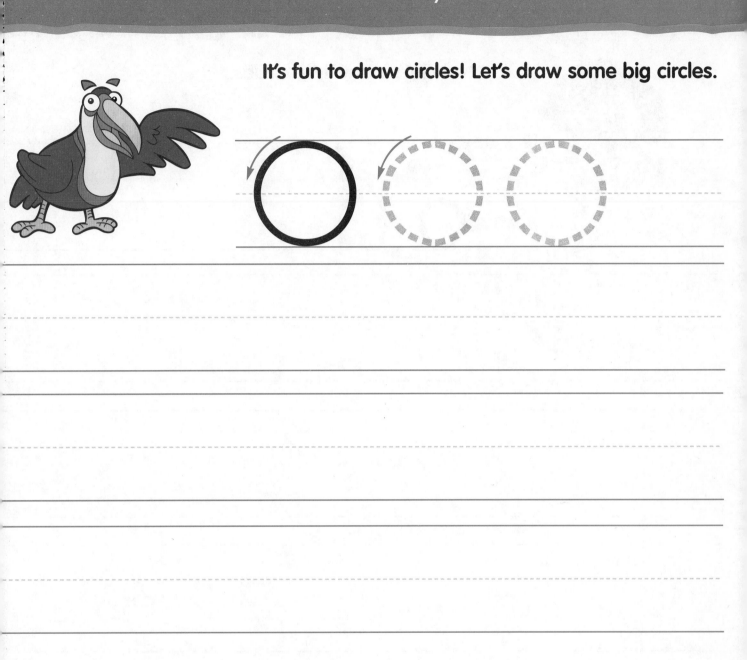

It's fun to draw circles! Let's draw some big circles.

The capital letters O and Q have big circles.

Now let's draw little circles.

The lowercase letter o is a little circle. Let's write it!

It's time to put it together! Write these letters, then finish writing the words.

O O O O

W W W W

o o o

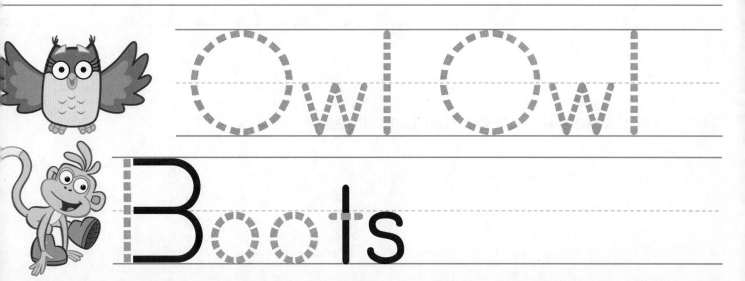

Owl Owl

Boots

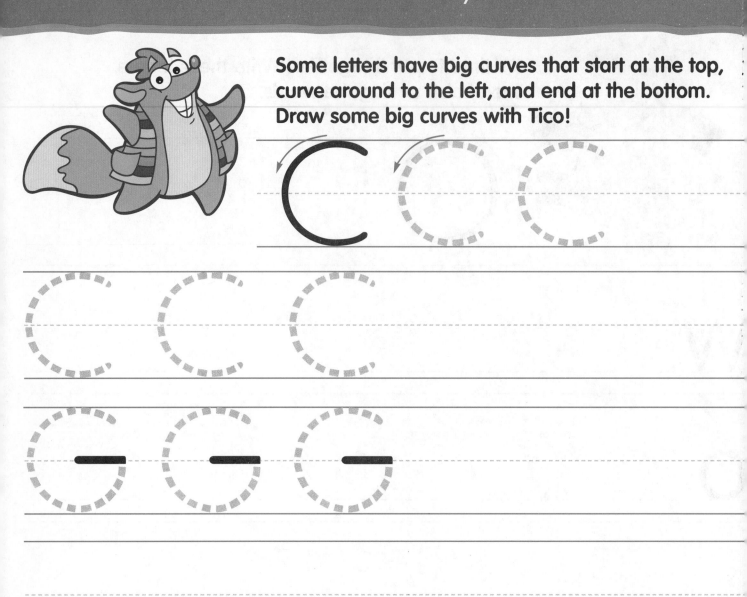

Some letters have big curves that start at the top, curve around to the left, and end at the bottom. Draw some big curves with Tico!

The capital letters **C** and **G** have big curves.

Now let's draw some small curves.

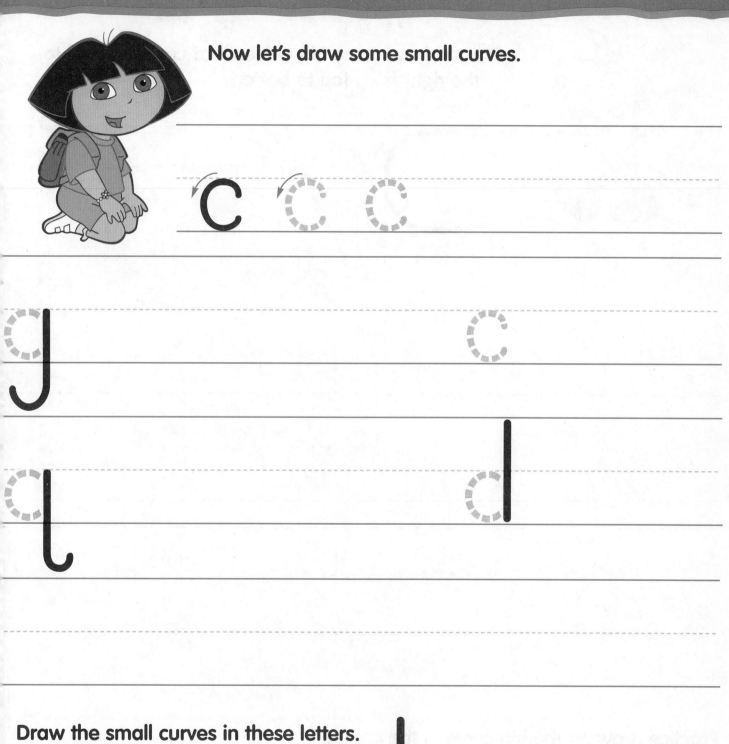

Draw the small curves in these letters.

Let's draw some big curves that curve around to the right from top to bottom.

Practice drawing the big curve in the capital D.

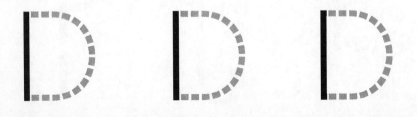

Now let's draw some small curves that curve around to the right from top to bottom.

Do you see the small curves in these letters? Great! Draw them.

Two curving shapes make the letter S.
Let's write the letter S.

Do you see how two curving shapes make capital S and lowercase s?
Great! Write more!

We can also end straight lines in a curve to make letters. The curve can be at the top or the bottom. Let's draw some long, straight lines with curves!

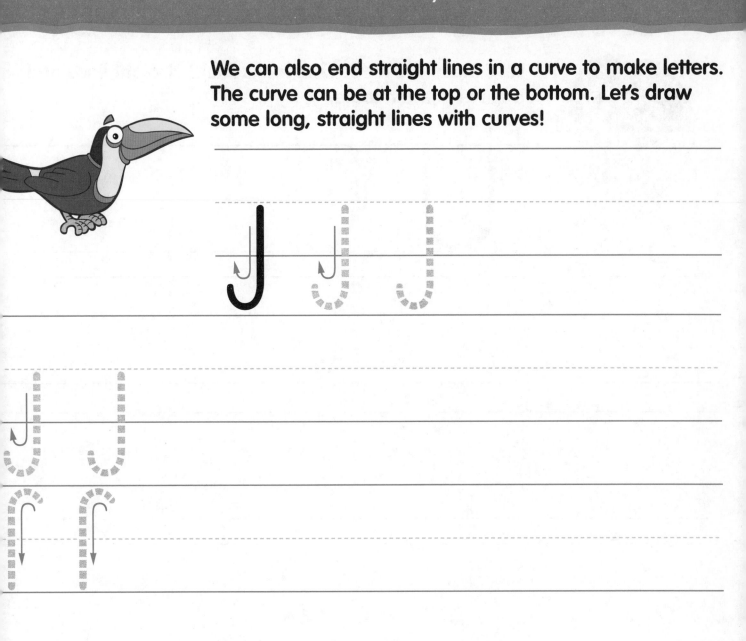

Here are some letters that end straight lines in a curve.

Let's make the letter **U**. It looks like 2 straight lines and a curve in the middle.

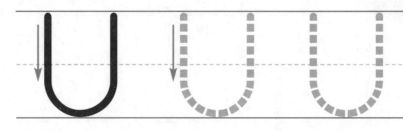

Write the capital letter U!

Some letters curve to the right then go straight. Draw these lines with Tico.

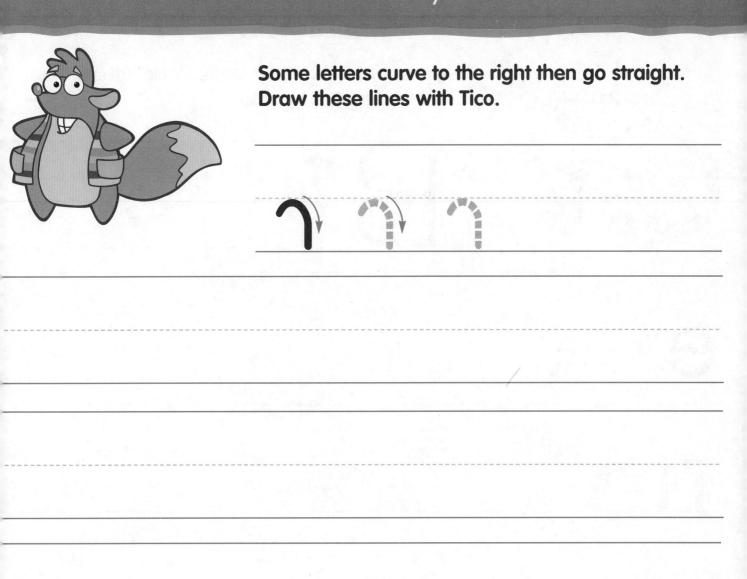

Look at the way curves and straight lines are used in these letters!

Help us put it together! Write these letters, then finish writing the words.

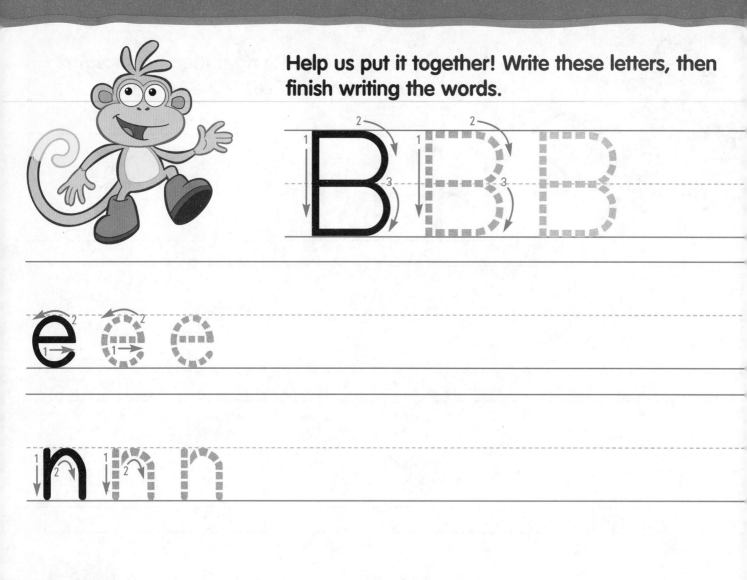

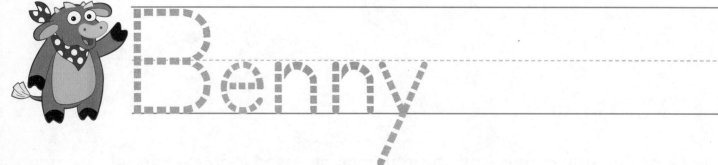

Look! We can write every letter of the alphabet using lines and curves! First, let's do capital letters.

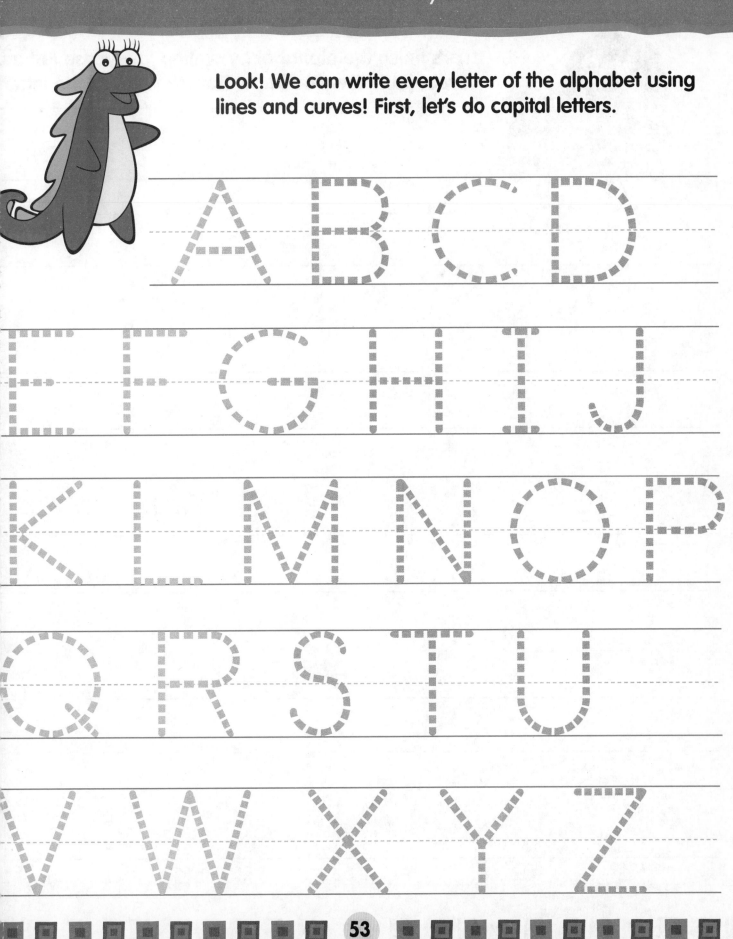

Let's finish the alphabet by writing lowercase letters
Great job! Now you know how to write all the letter

NUMBERS
Teach your child to:
- count in correct sequence 1-50
- trace and write numbers 1-20
- add numbers 1-10
- subtract numbers 1-10
- learn Spanish number words 1-20

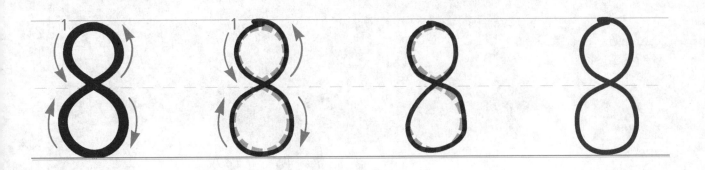

eight   ocho

Dora wants to practice writing numbers, but some numbers are missing. Can you help find them? Circle the hidden numbers.

Now my friends and I are exploring numbers. Will you explore numbers with us? Let's start with the number 1. Write the number 1.

Count how many.

one  uno

Boots sees 2 maracas. Practice writing the number 2.

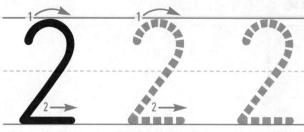

Count how many.

two **dos**

We have **3** friends in the Fiesta Trio.
Let's write the number **3**.

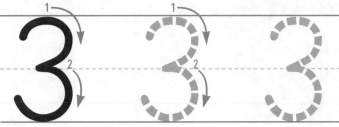

ount how many.

three        **tres**

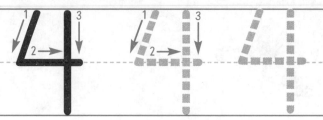

We see **4** ice cream cones.
Practice writing the number **4**.

Count how many.

four   **cuatro**

Tico has 5 toy cars. Write the number 5.

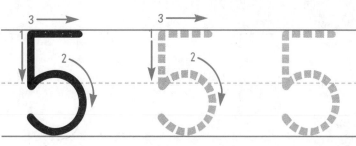

Count how many.

five   **cinco**

Let's write the numbers 1 through 5.

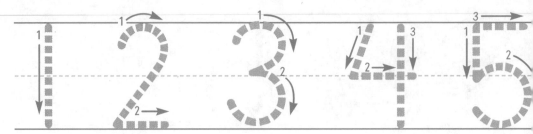

1 one		1 uno	2 two	2 dos	3 three	3 tres

4 four	4 cuatro	5 five	5 cinco

**Boots found 6 ducks at the duck pond.
Practice writing the number 6.**

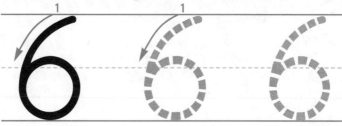

Count how many.

six   **seis**

Señor Tucan sees 7 nests. Let's write the number 7.

Count how many.

seven

siete

Isa has 8 colorful bows. Practice writing the number 8.

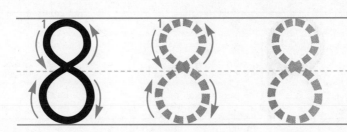

 count how many.

eight   **ocho**

Boots saw 9 scooters in a row! Practice writing the number

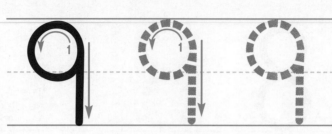

Count how many.

nine   **nueve**

We made it to 10!

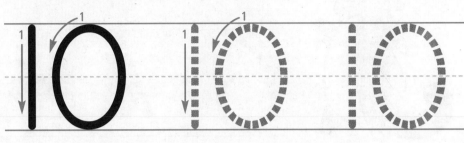

Count how many.

ten   **diez**

Lets write the numbers 6 through 10.

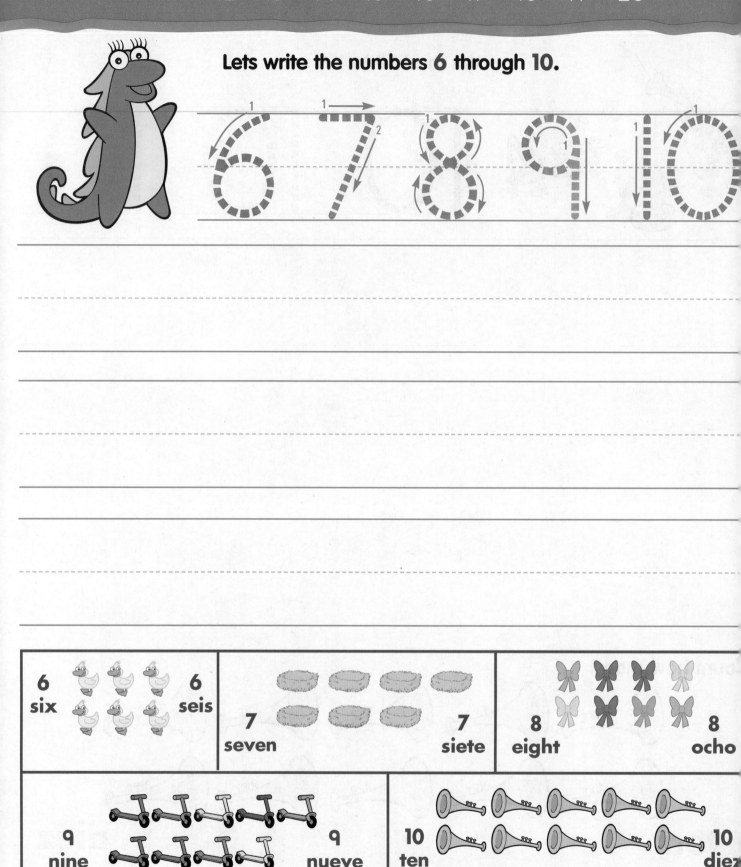

6
six

6
seis

7
seven

7
siete

8
eight

8
ocho

9
nine

9
nueve

10
ten

10
diez

I have 11 crayons. Help me write the number 11.

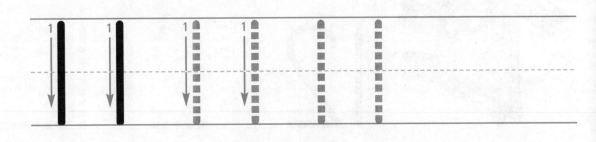

Count how many.

eleven　　　　　　　　　　**once**

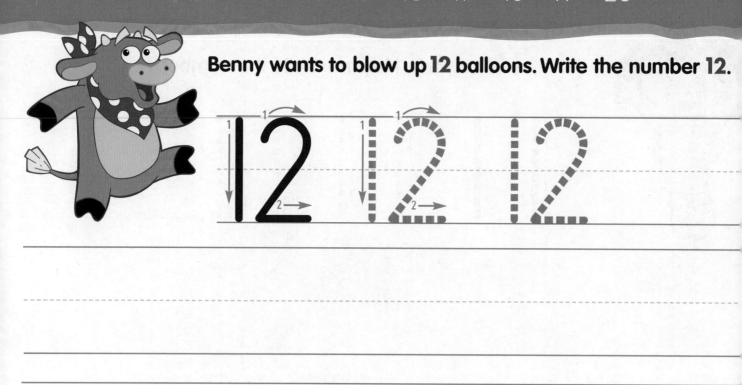

Benny wants to blow up 12 balloons. Write the number 12.

Count how many.

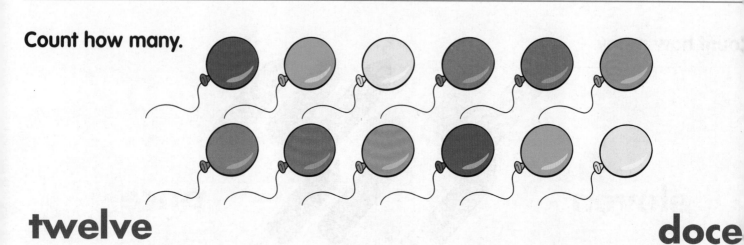

twelve

doce

Boots has 13 bouncy balls! Let's write the number 13.

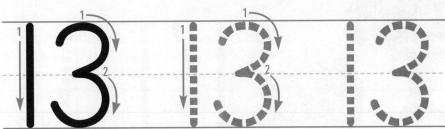

Count how many.

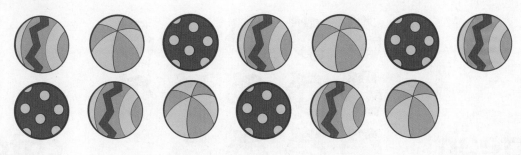

thirteen   **trece**

Tico wants to pick **14** nuts. Let's write the number 14

Count how many.

fourteen 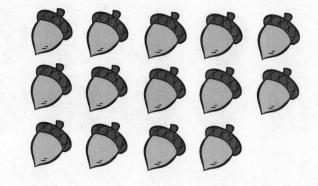 catorce

Boots and I caught 15 stars.
Practice writing the number 15.

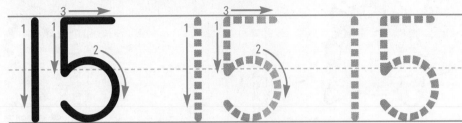

Count how many.

fifteen

quince

Let's write the numbers 11 through 15.

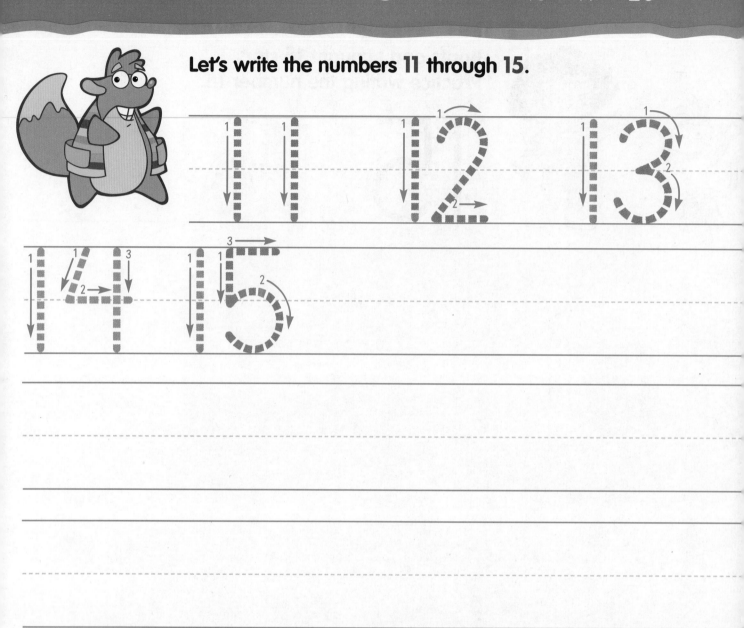

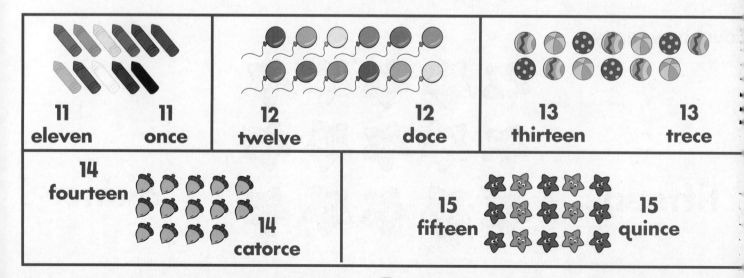

| 11 | 11 |
| eleven | once |

| 12 | 12 |
| twelve | doce |

| 13 | 13 |
| thirteen | trece |

14
fourteen

14
catorce

15
fifteen

15
quince

Isa needs to water 16 flowers. Write the number 16.

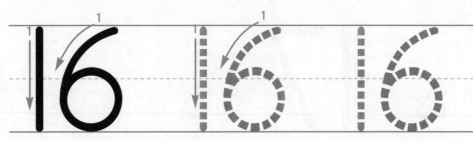

Count how many.

sixteen   **dieciséis**

Boots saw 17 cupcakes at the bakery!
Help Boots write the number 17.

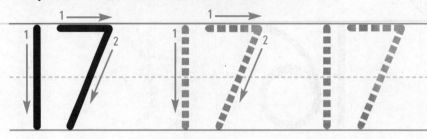

Count how many.

seventeen   **diecisiete**

I want to find 18 butterflies. Write the number 18.

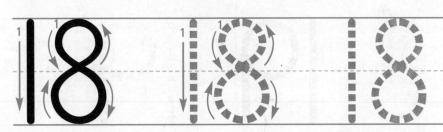

ount how many.

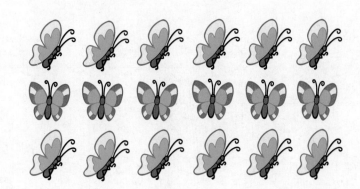

eighteen

dieciocho

Tico can blow 19 bubbles! Let's write the number 19.

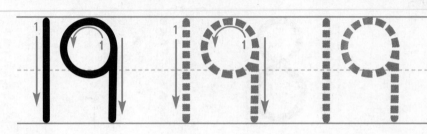

Count how many.

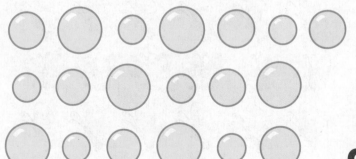

nineteen

diecinueve

We made it to 20! Hooray! Let's write the number 20.

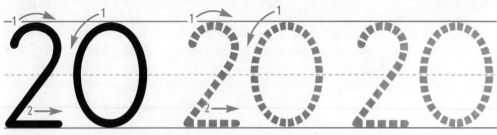

ount how many.

twenty

veinte

Practice writing the numbers 16 through 18.

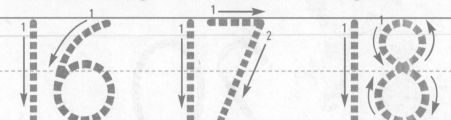

16
dieciseis

16
sixteen

17
diecisiete

17
seventeen

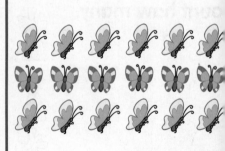

18
dieciocho

18
eighteen

Practice writing the numbers 19 through 20.

Thanks for helping us explore numbers. Gracias!

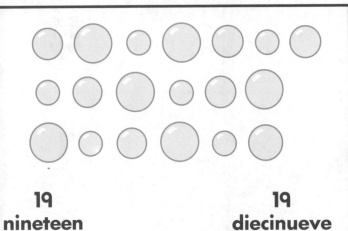

19
nineteen

19
diecinueve

20
twenty

20
veinte

Get ready for the star catching adventure!
Count the stars on the left then draw a line from
the stars to the correct number.

5

3

2

4

1

Now Boots and I are going on a star-catching adventure to Star Mountain. Will you be a Star Catcher with us? We'll need the special decoder inside this book. We can use it to see the hidden answers that the arrow is pointing to.

And don't forget to watch for Swiper the fox. If you him see, say, "Swiper, no swiping!"

The Map says we need to go through the Dark Forest and then over Turtle Stream. That's how we'll get to Star Mountain.

Look, stars! ¡Estrellas! Boots and I each caught 2 stars. Help us add my 2 stars to his 2 stars by counting all the stars we have together. Write the number and use the decoder to check your answer. Smart adding! Let's put the stars in my star pocket.

2 + 2 = _____

How many shoes do you see? Add my 2 white shoes and Boots' 2 red shoes.

2 + 2 = _____

It's too dark in the Dark Forest to see any stars. Boots didn't catch any stars, and neither did I.

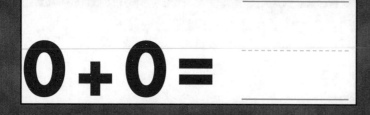

$$0 + 0 = \underline{\hspace{3cm}}$$

How many green stars do you see?

Did we catch any stars at all? No, we didn't. We need an Explorer Star to help us see in the dark. Do you know which Explorer Star can help us?

It's Glowy, the bright light Explorer Star! Glowy is shining so we can see the stars! Thanks, Glowy.

Boots and I each caught 1 purple star. Add them together.

1 + 1 = _____

Count all the stars.

2 + 1 = _____

And look! More stars to catch in the Dark Forest! How many blue stars are there? Count them and write the number.

How many stars are winking?

Let's add Glowy to the 4 blue stars we just caught in the Dark Forest.

4 + 1 = _____

Can you find another star hidden in the picture? Circle it.

Add each pair of numbers and write the total. Then draw a line to the star that shows the total.

3 + 2 = _____

3 + 4 = _____

2 + 1 = _____

4 + 2 = _____

6 + 4 = _____

3

5

7

10

6

I just caught 2 more stars and Boots caught 1. How many do we have together?

2 + 1 = _____

Oh, no. There are branches blocking the path! We need an Explorer Star to help us. Which Explorer Star can blow the branches out of our way?

It's Gusty, the windy Explorer Star! Gusty blew the branches out of our way. Thanks, Gusty!

Look, there are more stars! ¡Más estrellas! How many green stars do you see? Circle them and write the number.

How many red stars do you see?

You're right! There are no red stars!

Help us add Gusty to the 3 green stars we just caught.

$$3 + 1 = \rule{2cm}{0.4pt}$$

We just caught more stars! Boots caught 3 and I caught 2. How many did we catch together?

3 + 2 = _____

How many flowers and trees do you see?

3 + 2 = _____

Add each pair of numbers and write the total. Then draw a line to
the star that shows the total.

9 + 1 = _____

1 + 6 = _____

5 + 3 = _____

2 + 7 = _____

3 + 1 = _____

7

4

10

8

9

95

We made it to Turtle Stream! Boots caught 2 more stars on this side of the stream, but I didn't catch any. How many is that?

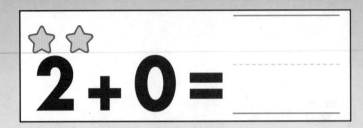

$$2 + 0 = \underline{\hspace{2cm}}$$

There are 2 turtles in the water and 1 out of the water. How many turtles are there all together?

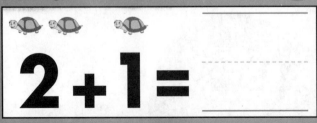

$$2 + 1 = \underline{\hspace{2cm}}$$

We need an Explorer Star to help us cross the water. Which Explorer Star can help us?

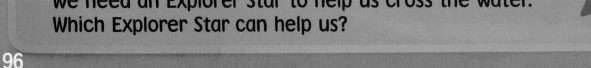

It's Saltador, the super jumping Explorer Star! Saltador helped us jump over Turtle Stream. Thanks, Saltador!

And look! There are pink stars on this side! How many pink stars do you see? Catch them, catch them! Circle them and write the number.

Now, let's add Saltador to the 5 pink stars we just caught.

$$5 + 1$$

I just caught 1 more star, but Boots didn't catch any. How many stars did we just catch all together?

$$1 \star \atop +0$$

Adding down is the same as adding across! Add these numbers then circle the correct answer below each problem.

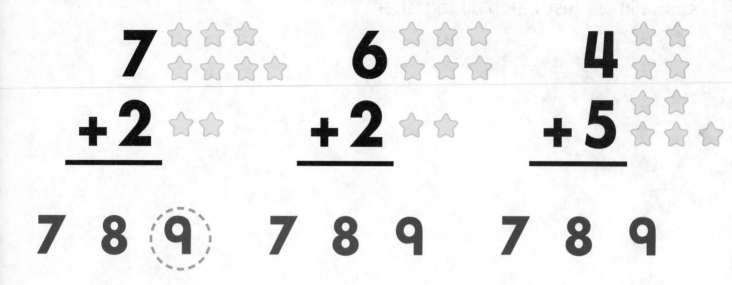

7
+2
---
7 8 (9)

6
+2
---
7 8 9

4
+5
---
7 8 9

1
+5
---
4 5 6

3
+3
---
4 5 6

We're almost to the top of Star Mountain. Look! More stars!
Boots caught 4 stars and so did I. How many is that all together?
Write the number and check your answer.

$$\begin{array}{r} 4 \\ + 4 \\ \hline \end{array}$$

How many stars can
you count on our path?

Uh, oh. I see Swiper. That sneaky
fox will try to swipe the stars
we caught! Say, "Swiper, no swiping!"

Thanks for helping us stop Swiper!

We made it to the top of Star Mountain! There are lots of stars to catch here. I caught 5 and so did Boots. Let's add them together.

5 + 5 = _____

Now count the fingers on my hand and the fingers on Boots' hand. How many?

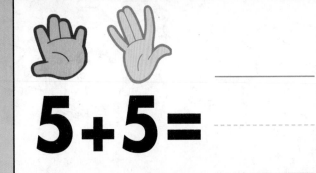

5 + 5 = _____

103

We caught so many stars today! Count and color all the stars we caught. How many did you count? Use your decoder to check your answer.

How many stars are winking?

How many stars did swiper get?

Thanks for helping! You're a great Star Catcher!

What kind of Explorer Star would you like to meet? Connect the dots from 1 to 10 and color the picture to finish your Explorer Star.

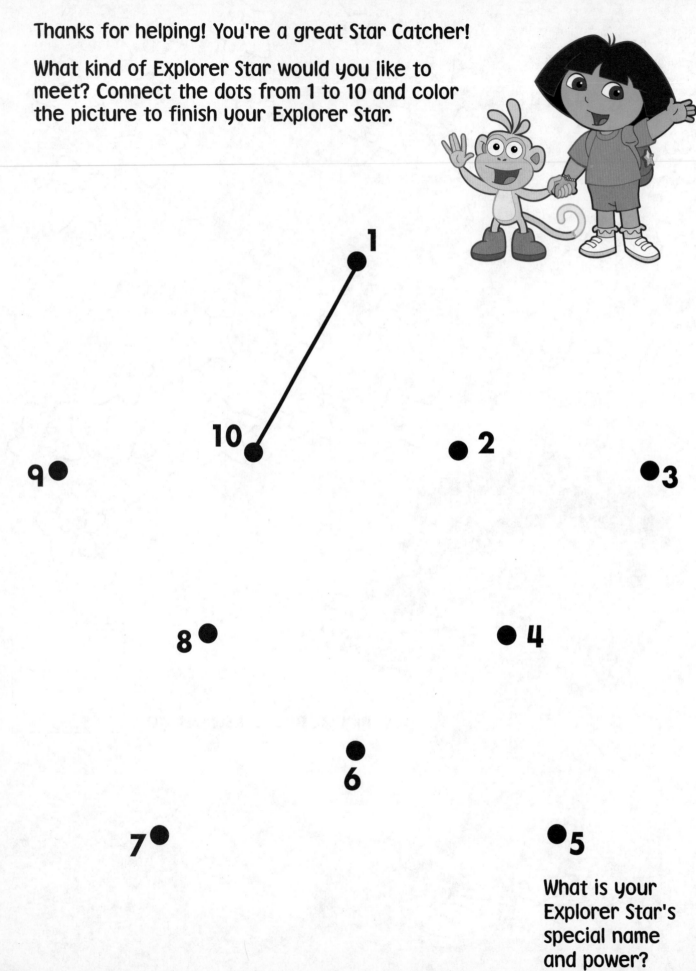

What is your Explorer Star's special name and power?

Flashcards

Directions:

1. Tear out each flashcard page.
2. Cut the flashcards apart on the dotted lines

1.

2.

Mix Up

Mix the number cards up and see if your child can put them back in the correct order. Try putting them in order backwards too. Take out a few cards and see if your child can guess which ones are missing. For younger children, start with the numbers 1-5 and then advance to higher numbers when you feel your child is ready.

Number Hunt

Choose 4 or 5 of the number cards and walk around the house with them. Encourage your child to find the numbers on common household items like a cereal box, a calendar, clothing, a tube of toothpaste or books. Make it a race to see who can find the number first. Or, take the number cards with you on a car trip and see if you can find the numbers in the community.

Add Away!

Help your child learn to add by choosing two cards with different numbers. Use small items like marshmallows, pretzels or pennies for counting so that your child can learn about one to one correspondence. Encourage your child to first count out the correct number of items and then help him/her add the items together like 3 pennies + 2 pennies = 5 pennies. Help your child to see which set has more and which set has less.

Now Boots and I are at the library. I'm going to check out 10 books. Boots wants to check out 10 books too. Will you help us? Great! We'll need the special decoder inside this book. We can use it to see the hidden answers where the arrow is pointing.

And keep an eye out for Swiper the fox. If you see him, say, "Swiper, no swiping!"

NEW BOOKS
YOU MAY CHECK OUT 2
NEW BOOKS

This is the New Book section! I want these 5 books, but the sign says I can only check out 2 new books. Circle the 2 books that I should keep, then count how many I need to put back. Write the number and use the decoder to check your answer.

$$5 - 2 = \underline{}$$

NEW BOOKS
YOU MAY CHECK OUT 2
NEW BOOKS

Smart subtracting!

Boots picked out 3 new books, but he has to put 1 of them back on the shelf. Mark an X on 1 book. Now write how many books Boots will have left after he puts the 1 book back.

3 - 1 = _____

Look! Here are some books about exploring! I wanted to check out all 6 books, but some of them are the same. Circle one copy of each book. Mark an X on the extra copies that are exactly the same. How many different books about exploring can I check out?

$$6 - 3 = \underline{\qquad}$$

Boots found 3 books about fire trucks, but he's already read all 3 of them. Mark an X on the books that Boots already read. How many are left? Write the number and check your answer.

3 - 3 = _____

Val the librarian is choosing some books to put out. We can help her. Subtract the numbers then draw a line to the book that shows the answer.

2 - 1 = _____

6 - 4 = _____

10 - 7 = _____

5 - 1 = _____

8 - 3 = _____

Boots founds 7 books about bouncy balls. He loves bouncy balls, especially red ones. Circle the 3 books about red bouncy balls. How many books are left?

$$7 - 3 = \underline{\hspace{2cm}}$$

Dora wants the green book. How many are left?

$$7 - 1 = \underline{\hspace{2cm}}$$

Boots also wants the book about yellow bouncy balls. Circle it and count how many books are left over.

$$4 - 1 = \text{\_\_\_}$$

Val helped me find 5 books in Spanish. If I put 3 of them back, how many books will I have left? Mark an X on 3 books and count how many are left.

$$5 - 3 = \underline{\qquad}$$

Uh, oh. There's Swiper! That sneaky fox wants to swipe 2 of my books! I have 7 books. If he took 2, how many would I have left? We can't let him swipe the books! Say, "Swiper, no swiping!"

$$7 - 2 = \underline{\hspace{3cm}}$$

Thanks for stopping Swiper.

Oh, no! Now Swiper is trying to swipe 2 of Boots' books! Boots has 6 books. If Swiper took 2, how many would Boots have left? Don't let Swiper take the books! Say, "Swiper, no swiping!"

6 - 2 = _____

What if he swiped 4?

6 - 4 = _____

Thanks for stopping Swiper.

Let's help Val sort these books. Subtract these numbers, then draw a line to the book that shows the correct answer.

 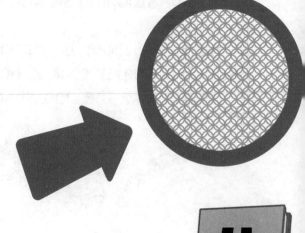

5 - 5 = _____

10 - 6 = _____

4 - 2 = _____

7 - 4 = _____

8 - 7 = _____

4

3

0

1

2

Here are 4 books about food. Boots likes bananas. Are any of these about bananas? Circle them and count how many other food books are left.

$$\begin{array}{r} 4 \\ -3 \\ \hline \end{array}$$

How many apples do you see? _____

Here's a whole section of books on boats. There are 9 boat books, but I only want the ones about little rowboats like mine! Find out how many books are about rowboats. Mark an X on the books that are not about rowboats. Count how many books are left.

9
-7
_____

Boots found one more book that he likes. That makes 10 books! But he changed his mind about 2 of them. How many books will Boots have left after he puts the 2 books back? Write the number and use the decoder to check your answer.

$$\begin{array}{r} 10 \\ -2 \\ \hline \end{array}$$

Val the librarian wants to find out how many books have been taken off each shelf. Will you help her? Great! Subtracting down is the same as subtracting across. Subtract, then circle the correct answer below each problem.

$$5 - 4$$

1 2 3

$$7 - 5$$

1 2 3

$$8 - 5$$

2 3 4

$$9 - 3$$

4 5 6

$$7 - 1$$

4 5 6

$$10 - 3$$

7 8 9

Boots likes books with tapes so he can listen and read along. He picked out 9, but decided he'll only take 2. How many does he need to put back?

$$\begin{array}{r} 9 \\ -2 \\ \hline \end{array}$$

There are 2 books with tapes that I like, but I think I'll only take 1 of them. How many books will I put back?

$$\begin{array}{r} 2 \\ -1 \\ \hline \end{array}$$

There's Swiper again. That sneaky fox will try to swipe my book with a tape. Say "Swiper, no swiping!"

Thanks for helping us stop Swiper! I had 1 book with a tape and Swiper didn't swipe it. So how many do I have left?

$$
\begin{array}{r}
1 \\
-\,0 \\
\hline
\end{array}
$$

How many books does swiper have?

We did it! Boots and I each picked out the 10 books we want to take home. Now we're going to check them out. Oops! Boots knocked 1 of his books off the counter. How many books does Boots have left on the counter?

$$\begin{array}{r} 10 \\ -1 \\ \hline \end{array}$$

Val the librarian wants to find out how many books have been taken off each shelf for the favorite books table. Let's help her. Subtract, then circle the correct answer below each problem.

$$\begin{array}{r} 8 \\ -1 \\ \hline \end{array}$$

7   8   9

$$\begin{array}{r} 8 \\ -4 \\ \hline \end{array}$$

3   4   5

$$\begin{array}{r} 6 \\ -1 \\ \hline \end{array}$$

5   6   7

$$\begin{array}{r} 10 \\ -2 \\ \hline \end{array}$$

6   7   8

$$\begin{array}{r} 9 \\ -2 \\ \hline \end{array}$$

5   6   7

$$\begin{array}{r} 6 \\ -5 \\ \hline \end{array}$$

0   1   2

Boots and I are going to my house to look at our books. We're taking the Math Problem path. Will you help us along the path? Great! Solve the problems to help us get to my house!

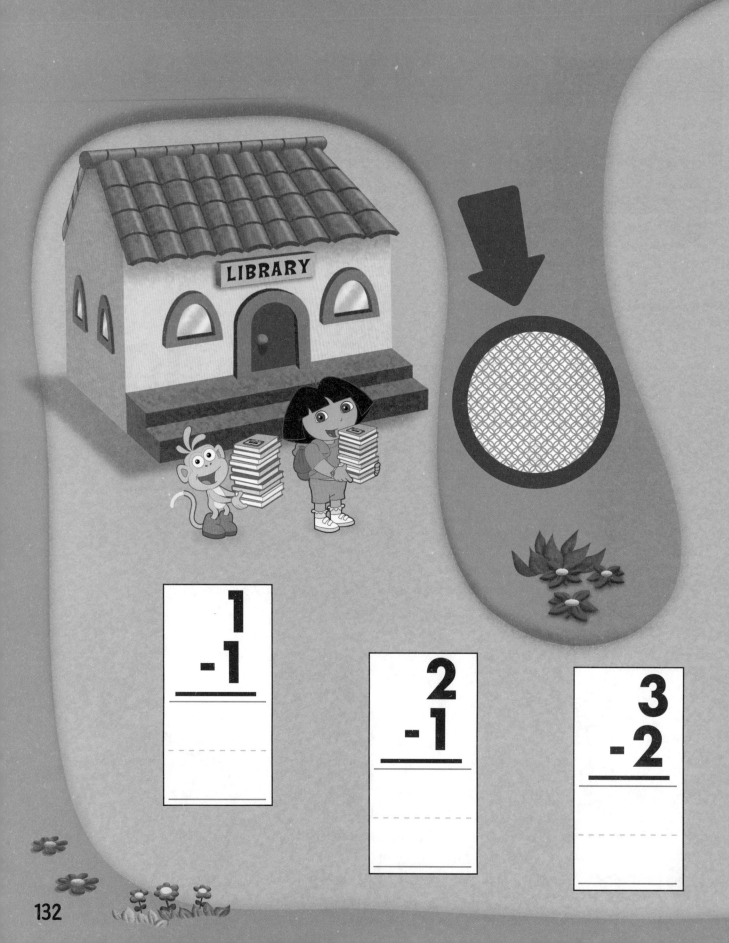

$$\begin{array}{r} 1 \\ -1 \\ \hline \end{array}$$

$$\begin{array}{r} 2 \\ -1 \\ \hline \end{array}$$

$$\begin{array}{r} 3 \\ -2 \\ \hline \end{array}$$

$$\begin{array}{r} 6 \\ -4 \\ \hline \end{array}$$

$$\begin{array}{r} 7 \\ -3 \\ \hline \end{array}$$

$$\begin{array}{r} 8 \\ -5 \\ \hline \end{array}$$

$$\begin{array}{r} 5 \\ -2 \\ \hline \end{array}$$

$$\begin{array}{r} 9 \\ -4 \\ \hline \end{array}$$

$$\begin{array}{r} 4 \\ -2 \\ \hline \end{array}$$

We had such a great time picking out books at the library. Thanks for helping us. Do you have a library card? Connect the dots from 1 to 10 to make a library card for our library! Write your name on the line and color the card.

Library Card

Name

Great job!

OPPOSITES
Teach your child to:
- understand concepts of location and direction
- develop spatial skills
- follow a simple map

Reveals hidden answers!

Includes a
SPECIAL
DECODER!

Help add some color to the picture!
Draw two grey clouds UP in the sky.
Draw two orange flowers DOWN near Dora's feet.
Draw a blue sky OVER Dora's head.
Draw the green grass UNDER Dora's feet.
Draw a red hat ON Dora's head.
Draw a yellow ball IN Boots' hand.
Great job!

Hi! I'm Dora and this is my friend Boots. I lost my flute. Will you help us find it? Great! We'll need the special decoder included in this book. We can use it to see the hidden answers that the Arrow is pointing to. And keep an eye out for Swiper the fox. If you see him, say, "Swiper, no swiping!"

137

The Map says I left my flute at Play Park. We need to go over the Troll Bridge and then across the Duck Pond. That's how we'll get to Play Park.

We made it to the Troll Bridge, but who is that under it? Circle who you see under the bridge. Use our decoder to check the answer.

The Grumpy Old Troll won't let us go over his bridge unless we solve his riddle. Can you help us solve it? Circle the answer to this riddle.

"Some are up and some are down, to find them all just look around. Look for blue and look for red, look under the tree and over your head."

Smart looking! Now we can go over the bridge. Which path should we take? Draw a line to show the path that goes over the bridge.

A

B

Help me match these things that are over, under, up and down. Draw a line between the ones that are the same.

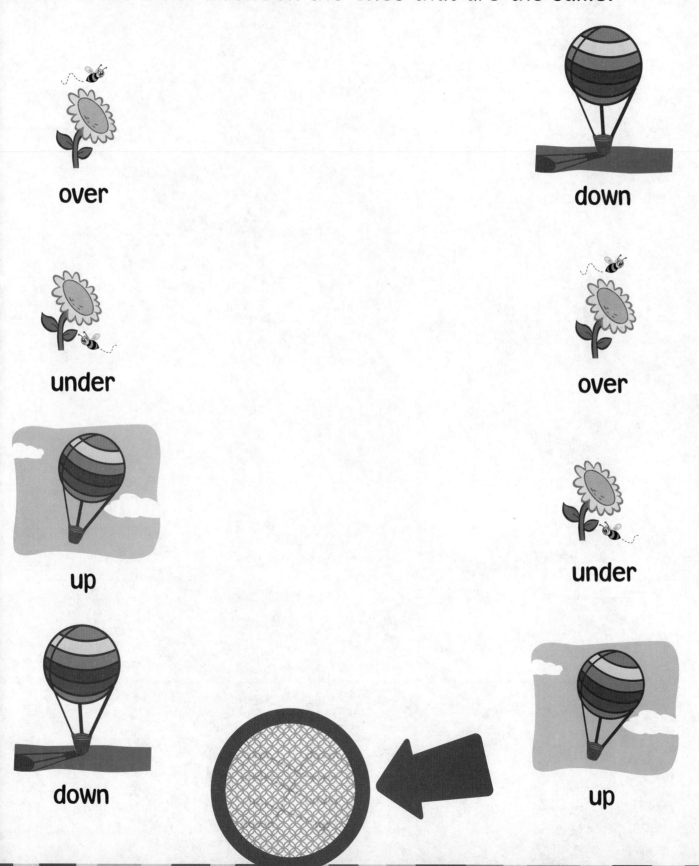

over

down

under

over

up

under

down

up

Next we need to cross the Duck Pond. The boat out of the pond is broken, but the one in the pond is not. Circle the boat that we should use.

in

out

Uh oh, I think someone is hiding behind the bush. Color who you see behind the bush.

That sneaky fox will try to swipe our boat!
Say, "Swiper, no swiping!"

We stopped Swiper!

Hey, look at all the ducks in the pond. Will you help us count the ducks swimming in front of us? Write the number then use the decoder to check the answer.

We made it across the Duck Pond. One of us is still in the boat and the other is out. Color the one out of the boat.

Will you help me sort these birds?
Great!
Circle the words below the two
pictures that are the same in
each row.

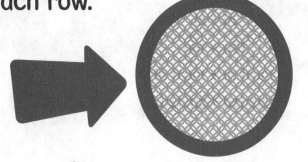

in

out

in

in

out

out

in front

in front

behind

behind

in front

behind

Now we have to go to Play Park. I see two paths, but only one path leads to Play Park. Should we take the path on the left or the path on the right? Color the sign that shows which way we should go.

LEFT

RIGHT

There is Play Park! It's high on the hill. I can see the sandbox.
What else do you see?

Circle the play things on the hill. Put an X on the one that is off the hill.

Look, I found some balls! Help me show where they are compared to the tree stump. Draw a line from each ball to the word that describes where it is.

on

right

left

off

We made it to Play Park. I don't see my flute, but I see something in the sandbox and something on the slide. Color them!

Play Park is full of places to look, like behind and in front of the horse. Behind and in front are opposites. They are completely different from each other. Draw a line to connect the other pairs of opposites.

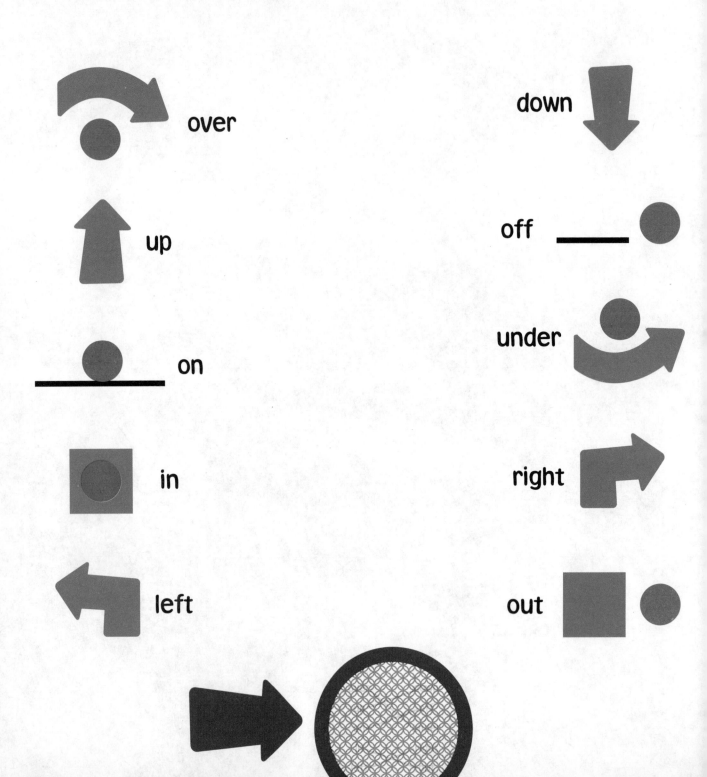

over

down

up

off

on

under

in

right

left

out

There's one more place to look. What do you see under the swings? Circle it!

We did it! We found my flute. Hooray! Now lets play!
Trace the words.

Thanks for helping me find my flute!